Temples

Great temples were built by the Inca, Aztec, and Maya for religious ceremonies. Often they were built in the shape of a pyramid. The ruins of many of these temples are still standing.

Inca House

The Inca built their houses from stone blocks. The blocks were so carefully cut that the stones stayed together without any kind of cement. The roofs were made from weeds and grass.

Inca, Aztec, Maya

Table of Contents

Illustrated by Elizabeth Adams

©1999 Edupress, Inc. • P.O. Box 883 • Dana Point, CA 92629

ISBN 1-56472-211-2
Printed in USA

Activity Guide

Look for the at the top of the coloring page

Look and Find

Page 15. Find and circle the parts of the dresses that are embroidered.

Page 21. Find and circle the objects that were made from the stone obsidian.

Page 29. Find the flute and make a blue circle around it. Make a red circle around the ocarina. Make a green circle around the drum.

Page 30. Find and circle the ball and hoop that are part of the game being played.

Complete the Picture

Page 4. Draw and color stones on all the houses to match the house in front.

Page 7. Draw and color a sack of seeds hanging around the planter's neck.

Page 9. Complete the picture by drawing and coloring plants on every terrace.

Page 28. Draw and color a sun rising above the mountains in the background.

Color to Match

Page 11. Color the three finished tortillas a light brown.

Page 12. Color the yarn the woman is using to weave the fabric red.

Page 24. Color the reed sail on the boat a pale yellow.

Page 26. Color the clay figure in shades of red, and brown, and gray.

Unscramble the Words

Page 5. Unscramble the words for the materials used to build an Aztec home.

sgars   dmu   dobae ckbris

Page 10. Unscramble the names of food the Incas, Aztecs, and Mayans ate.

totaesop   tenuspa   vocdoaa

Page 14. Unscramble the words for clothing worn by Aztec men.

eelthocbrhc   pace   dlasasn

Page 21. Unscramble the names of materials used to make the Inca chieftan's clothes and jewelry.

logd   lowo   tocotn

Aztec Home

Aztec homes were made of adobe bricks cemented together with mud. The houses had grass roofs. The rounded stone building was built as a sweat house, where people would take a bath.

Mayan House

A traditional Mayan house was called a na. The walls were made of poles. Sometimes the walls were covered with mud. The roofs were thatched reeds, grass, or palm leaves.

Planting

Aztec farmers planted their crops with simple tools. A wooden stick was used to loosen soil and to make a hole for the seeds. Seeds were kept in a bag hanging around the planter's neck, and they were dropped into the ground by hand.

Chinampas

The Aztecs built *chinampas* in shallow swamp areas. The chinampa was a plot of planting land created from water plants and soil piled behind woven fences, making an "island" in the swamp.

Farming Terraces

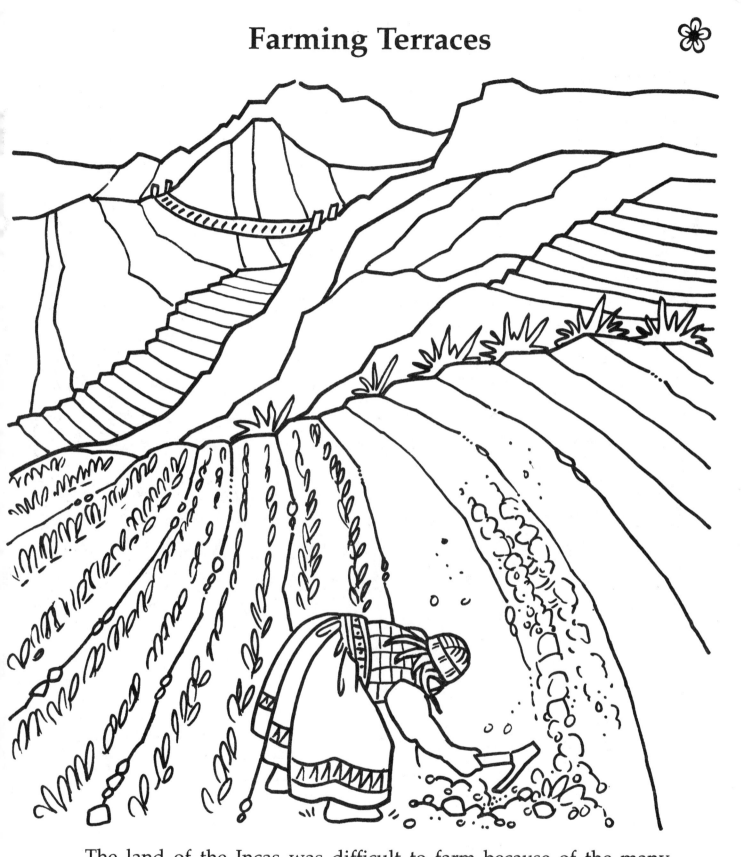

The land of the Incas was difficult to farm because of the many mountains. By creating terraces, or flat areas, in the mountainside, the Incas were able to create more farmland.

Food

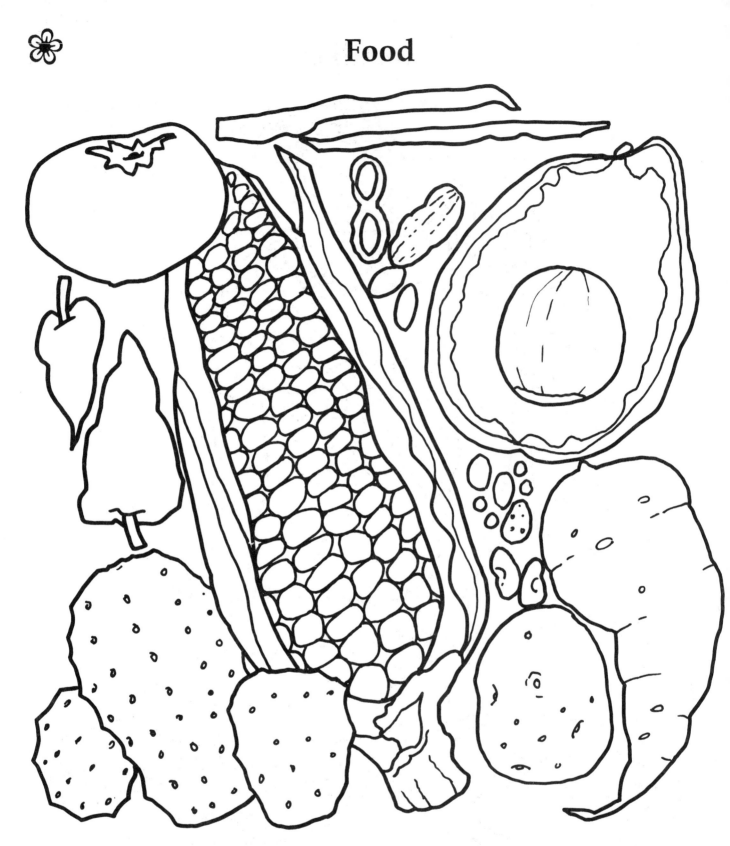

The diet of the Inca, Aztec, and Maya consisted mainly of vegetables, grains, and roots, which they gathered or grew. Among the foods they ate were beans, corn, potatoes, peppers, avocados, and peanuts. Fish and meat were eaten once in a while.

Tortillas

Hand-ground corn made into flat breads called tortillas was a food eaten every day by the Inca, Aztec, and Maya. The tortillas were baked on a flat stone over a fire.

Backstrap Loom

The Incas, Aztecs, and Mayas all wove fabrics on a backstrap loom.
One end of the loom was tied to a post or a tree, and the other end was
looped to create a strap around the weaver's body.

Inca Clothing

The clothing of the Incas was made from wool and cotton. The Incas used fabrics that had many colorful designs. Each region of the Inca Empire had its own style of headdress.

Aztec Clothing

The Aztecs made most of their clothing from cotton or a plant fiber called maguey. Men wore a breechcloth, a cape, and sandals. Women wore a skirt and blouse. Wealthier people had more decoration and color on the clothing they wore.

Maya Clothing

Most Mayan clothing was made of cotton. Men wore a loincloth with long ends hanging down in front and back. Women wore a straight dress, called a huipil, which was embroidered with colorful designs. The huipil is still worn by Mayan women today.

Feather Work

The Aztecs were especially known for elaborate feather work done on fans, shields, and clothing. They used the feathers of parrots and other tropical birds.

Masks

Masks were used in the Inca, Aztec, and Mayan cultures. They were made of many materials, including wood and gold. Some were mosaics made of jade or other stone.

Inca Chieftain

The Inca chieftain, or Tapa Inca, wore clothes woven from fine wool or cotton. He would also wear gold arm bands and earrings. The Tapa Inca would only wear each piece of clothing one time.

Inca Warrior

An Inca warrior wore a quilted tunic and a shield made of wood and cotton on his back. When a warrior performed well in battle, he might be awarded better battle clothing by his leader.

Aztec Chieftain

The leader of the Aztecs was called the Tlatoani. Each new chief was chosen by a high council or committee from one of the important Aztec families. Like the nobles or upper class, he would wear fine clothes, jewels, and elaborate headdresses.

Aztec Warrior

An Aztec warrior wore a beautifully colored costume. He also wore
a feathered headdress. A warrior carried a spear and a war club made
of wood and a glass-like stone called obsidian.

Maya Chieftain

Maya cities were probably led by both priests and chieftains. A Maya chieftain had both political and religious powers. The chieftain wore a headdress made of quitzal feathers. He carried a staff and a feather fan.

Maya Warrior

A Maya warrior wore clothing made from the hide of a jaguar, an animal that the Maya thought was sacred. The jaguar symbolized strength and courage. He also wore a feather headdress and earrings.

Reed Boat

The Incas used boats made from reeds for fishing and travel. They sailed on major rivers, Lake Titicaca, and along the ocean coast. The boats were made by lashing reeds together. Some had sails that were also made from reeds.

Dugout Canoe

The Aztec cities had canals filled with water instead of roads. The Aztecs used dugout canoes for travel, fishing, and to transport goods. The canoes were made from one log with the center burned out.

Clay Figures

The Maya were very skilled in the art of sculpture. Human figures were carved from stone or formed from clay. The small clay sculptures often represented one of the Maya's many gods.

Sacred Serpent

The sacred serpent was an important symbol in the Mayan culture. It appeared carved on columns and buildings, in funeral and religious sculpture, and on ceremonial headdresses.

Raymi Festival

During the Incan Raymi festival, the Tapa Inca and his relatives would go to an appointed place to wait for the sun to rise. The Tapa Inca would then pour wine onto the earth for the sun to drink.

Musical Instruments

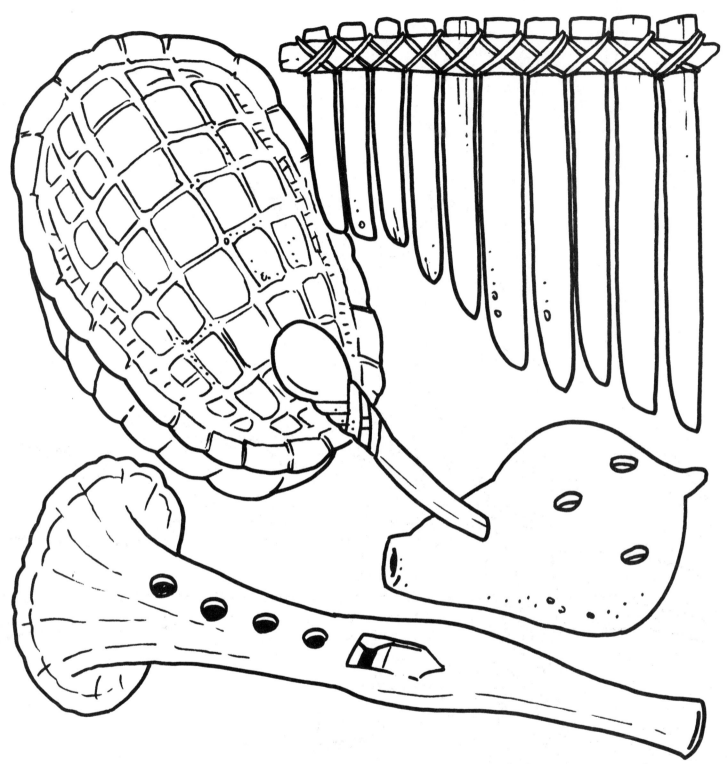

The musical instruments used by the Aztecs during ceremonies included wind and percussion instruments. Flutes and pear-shaped ocarinas were made of wood or clay. Drums were made of wood and tortoise shell. Musicians also used rattles made of clay or dried gourds.

Tiachtli

Tiachtli was a ball game played by both the Aztecs and the Maya. It was played on a large court. Players would try to put a rubber ball through a hoop mounted on one of the court walls, using only their elbows and hips.

Volador

In an Aztec form of entertainment, four men dressed as birds jumped from a wooden platform mounted to a tall pole. The platform turned around, making the men "fly" around the pole thirteen times before they reached the ground.

Patolli

Patolli was an Aztec gambling game using counters or dried beans on a cross-shaped playing board. Some Aztecs believed that it was also a fortune-telling game. They thought that where the beans fell on the board would tell the players about the future.